A LEGEND IN MY OWN MIND

The Road to Overcoming Hopeless Situations

Wesley Cole

MARIGOLD PRESS BOOKS
A division of International School of Story

Copyright © 2023 Wesley Cole
ISBN: 978-1-942923-71-8
Library of Congress Control Number: 2023924725

All rights reserved. No portion of this book may be reproduced, stored in a retrieval system, or transmitted in any form or by any means–electronic, mechanical, photocopy, recording, scanning, or other–except for brief quotations in critical reviews or articles, without the prior written permission of the author.

Published in Savannah, Georgia by Marigold Press Books, a division of International School of Story.

Marigold Press Books titles may be purchased in bulk for educational, business, fund-raising, or sales promotional use. For information, please email marigoldpressbooks@gmail.com.

Fonts licensed for commercial use.
Cover Art and Book Design by Sarah Chang.

A LEGEND IN MY OWN MIND

The Road to Overcoming
Hopeless Situations

Dedication

I dedicate this book to my mom,
Thelma Rambo, also known as "Rambo."

And to all those who struggle
with the journey of addiction.

Contents

Introduction _____ 9

1. The Timid Legend _____ 11
2. Our Place of Violence and Belonging _____ 15
3. Our Streets of Crime _____ 21
4. The Unraveling of the Family _____ 27
5. The Chaos of Adult Life Begins _____ 31
6. The Allure of Drugs and Alcohol _____ 37
7. The Process of Recovery _____ 41

Are You Ready? _____ 50
    My Prayer for You _____ 51
    The Serenity Prayer _____ 51

About the Author _____ 52

Introduction

In the depths of despair, when all hope seemed lost, I embarked on a journey that would ultimately redefine my existence. *A Legend in My Own Mind: The Road to Overcoming Hopeless Situations* is a candid exploration of my tumultuous life, chronicles of the battles fought and the victories won against seemingly insurmountable odds. From a childhood marred by violence and instability, to a life plagued by addiction, incarceration, homelessness, and fractured relationships, this memoir unearths the raw truth of my own relentless pursuit of redemption.

Through the highs and lows, the triumphs and setbacks, I invite you to join me on this transformative quest of self-discovery, resilience, and grace, which allowed me to find the strength to conquer the most daunting of circumstances. It is a testament to the unwavering presence of a divine force. It is a journey that I have traveled, bearing witness to the remarkable resilience of the human spirit and the inexplicable ways in which God's hand extends to protect us amidst life's darkest trials. This is a tale of the unyielding power of faith and the transformative grace that emerges even from the depths of despair.

You will see revealed in every twist and turn the majestic hand of God safeguarding my life, offering solace in the face of anguish and guiding me towards a profound understanding of this resilience that resides within us all. It is the journey of seeing God's protective hand, even in the most unimaginable of traumas—a journey that left me forever changed, forever grateful, and forever in awe of the presence of God that intertwines with our human existence.

ONE

The Timid Legend

In the depths of my earliest memories, violence and chaos reigned. The air was thick with the stench of alcohol and the echoes of raucous parties and bitter arguments. I was three or four years old when the world revealed its tragic face to me. I can still vividly recall the sight of my mother wielding shot glasses as weapons, striking my father's head, crimson streams flowing from his wounds. Terrified, I fled into the streets, tears streaming down my face, a helpless witness to the destruction unfolding before my young eyes.

My upbringing was shaped by the firm grip of this controlling mother, a woman who carried pistols in her bag and between her breasts. I was her fourth child, who thought of myself as a legend.

I was good at boxing, football, and running. Good at everything I did. I always wanted to be the best, and even though I was not always number one, I was always a close second or third. This made me feel like a loser. This made me quit as soon as I felt I had to compete for a position. I would simply say to myself, "I don't need to do this, I am already the best." I did not want to look like a failure at anything. I needed to measure up to this strong woman, my mother!

After basking in the glory of being the baby boy for seven years, my little brother came along. A desperate need for recognition developed within me. Perhaps it was jealousy that brewed within me, as I was no longer the center of attention. Needing to be seen, I began acting out, seeking solace in the numbing embrace of alcohol—a habit that would haunt me in the years to come.

It was during second grade that I first played truant, driven by the fear of being the last one to enter the classroom, subjected to the scrutinizing gazes of my peers. I could not endure the thought of not being the first, the best, the leader. I could not be last. Fear gripped me, and I scurried back home and concealed myself behind the couch, hidden from the world.

My step-father and uncle found me cowering behind the couch, where I had sought refuge from the daunting corridors of the school. With a blend of sternness and understanding, they plucked me from my hiding place, leading me back to the very battleground I had attempted to flee. But this act of rescue had an unintended aftermath, carving a scar deeper than my original fears. Facing the principal's piercing gaze became a harrowing ordeal, a terror that surpassed even the prospect of venturing into the classroom I had evaded. The weight of my dread swelled, magnifying every step of the journey that lay ahead, my heart gripped with newfound insecurity and embarrassment.

Now it really became easy to skip school. If I didn't get A's and B's, I'd skip school. When I got a C in geometry, I didn't want anyone to see or think I couldn't do the math and decided to fail rather than face that. I'd skip school and justify it to myself—it was a choice I made and not the weakness of my not being able to do math.

This fear, being so sensitive, was amplified by my shyness. It seemed there were two sides of me—a true Gemini. Not that I understood this at all, it was so confusing. How could I be a hero, a legend in my mind, yet be so terrified?

The first time I didn't have the heart to do something was when I was seven years old. Alastair, my big brother, was in a fight and the boys were beating him up. I just stood there and cried. This haunted me. Where was The Legend? Number One? At that moment, I saw the cowardice in myself, intensifying my fear of being less than. It would drive me to do some crazy things in the years to come.

TWO
Our Place of Violence and Belonging

In the grand tapestry of time, 1963 emerges as a pivotal stitch, a date that transcends the confines of mere chronology to imprint itself on the very fabric of my memory. Though I was young, I sensed the weight carried by that year. President Kennedy, a name synonymous with greatness, had etched his mark on my mind, an emblem of promise and leadership. The world seemed to hold its breath in his presence. And then, as if orchestrated by the hands of destiny, news of his assassination echoed through the airwaves, shattering the fragile cocoon of my understanding. In that moment, the magnitude of loss surged through me.

But fate's cruel irony wasn't content with casting only one shadow upon that day. Amidst the tremors of a nation in mourning, I found myself standing in the heart of a street corner, the scene set for a drama far removed from the angry moments in my home. It was a realm of shadowy alliances and unrestrained violence, where the boundaries of law seemed absent. It was an encounter with the world of gangs.

The air hummed with tension; an unease gripped my heart. I witnessed the faces of anger, the clashing of factions vying for power, and I, the spectator, held within me the realization that innocence had no place within this space.

I was a mere eight years old when I witnessed a boy on our block being mercilessly beaten. Blood spilled onto the ground, further staining the innocence of my youth.

 Looking back, it was a day when the universe seemed to fold in upon itself, when history's hand reached out to touch the present. It was a day that shattered illusions, sweeping away the veil that had hidden the world's complexity from my eyes. The day, when President Kennedy was murdered and the chaos unfolded on the streets, two stories were woven together by the threads of uncertainty. In the end, that year would forever mark a turning point, a crossroads where I was forced to confront the intricacies of a world far beyond my youthful imaginings.

I soon learned the world I inhabited in Toledo, Ohio was notorious, and our family name was revered. No one dared to challenge my mother, my uncles, or any member of our household. It was a world where we, the boys, were raised to fight—whether in the clubs or on the unforgiving streets. Fear and aggression melded within me, transforming me into a bully haunted by cowardice. I wore a mask of toughness, emulating my mother's fiery disposition and repelled others with my explosive anger.

Tragedy struck again when I was eleven years old, robbing me of my eldest brother, Alastair. He succumbed to an asthma attack, his fragile health a constant burden. At the time, our mother lay in a hospital bed suffering with a stomach ailment, and in her grief, she placed blame on my stepfather and on the hospital itself.

She never recovered from his loss, plunging into a deep depression that unleashed a torrent of verbal abuse upon us, her own children. "I should've flushed you all down the toilet when I had you," she uttered drunkenly, her words laced with pain. Though she never intended to harm us, her anguish consumed her, yet she did her best in her own way. She always ended with the words, "I love you." My stepfather, too, tried his hardest, ensuring we lacked for nothing.

Alastair's absence left a gaping hole in our lives, prompting us to move to a different neighborhood in search of solace. In my mind, I always wondered what my life would have been like if Alastair had lived. He was our hero. He was so smart, an artist, and he was loved by the entire neighborhood. The impact of this tragedy seeped into my soul, poisoning my path through sixth grade and beyond as alcohol and drugs became my companions.

I continued to bear witness to the facets of humanity that lurked in the darkness. Prejudice, that insidious companion, had stealthily woven itself into the very fiber of my life. The Black Panthers, both feared and respected, took their place in the unfolding drama in my neighborhood. Their presence painted the air with whispers of defiance and dreams of equality, casting a spotlight on the intricate dance between hope and frustration characterizing those times.

And yet, fate's hand was not satisfied with one sorrowful note. In the same year, another tragic chord echoed through history's halls in 1968. Our greatest symbol of freedom, Martin Luther King Jr., was assassinated. It was not only the blacks that wept, wrenched in tears and pain, it was whites, it was all of us. The shock waves reverberated through our souls, carving yet another scar into our collective psyche.

Later that year, Bobby Kennedy, the torch bearer of his fallen brother's legacy, fell victim to the same malevolent force that had claimed President Kennedy's life. Here was a man who dared to tread the path of Civil Rights, his strides infused with the spirit of progress for African Americans. The loss was a blow to our fragile optimism, a reminder that even the brightest flames can be extinguished in a moment's breath.

As these seismic events unfurled against the backdrop of my tender thirteen years, my own landscape resembled anything but tenderness. The allure of rebellion had entangled itself around my being, guiding me down a path strewn with marijuana, theft, and the allure of pills and wine.

The school bell's chime now played second fiddle to the rush of chemical indulgence, while lies and manipulation became an art I mastered with astonishing dexterity. In the eyes of adults, I was a smart, well-mannered youth, while my true self lurked in the shadows, shrouded in secrecy.

Fear of discovery forged alliances with cunning, and soon, I had a circle of young accomplices, formed under my tutelage, drawn together by the promise of immediate gratification and the thrill of forbidden fruit. Innocence seemed a distant memory, replaced by the exhilarating rush and intoxicating allure of the darker side of life.

I found myself thrust into the midst of two murder trials. One friend's stepfather took the life of his mother, forever shattering any semblance of normalcy in their household. In a neighboring block, another friend met his demise at the hands of his own brother.

Then, one fateful day, my mother followed through on her chilling words. She had endured a severe beating at the hands of my stepfather, and the anger and pain within her reached a breaking point. She announced to us, her children, her intentions: "I am about to go and shoot this Motherf. Just call the police when I do this." We pleaded with her, begged her not to go through with it, but she silenced us with her commanding tone. "Shut up and do what I tell you all to do," she snapped. With unwavering determination, she walked towards the room where he sat in his chair.

Gunshots pierced the air as she unleashed her fury, and he tumbled out of the door, crashing over the banister. He survived this time, choosing not to press charges for the assault he had endured. Instead, my mother faced charges for possessing a weapon, leading to her incarceration and subsequent participation in AA meetings during her one-year work release program.

I didn't know it at the time, but this same program would save my life in the years to come.

THREE
Our Streets of Crime

Growing up in the midst of this violence, continued to affect every aspect of my existence. It rooted itself deeply into the fabric of my neighborhood, flickered on our television screens, and erupted in the streets where my cousins resided. I was angry. My attitude against the white establishment raged within me.

The increasing number of horrifying incidents in my neighborhood accumulated, adding to my anger, like the time my cousin's husband was mercilessly rammed into another car because of a fight. And there was the haunting memory of a man struck in the head with a parking sign, his life extinguished right before my young eyes. Violence became an inescapable companion, a constant reminder of the harsh realities of the world.

As I entered high school, the allure of alcohol and drugs entangled me further. Acid, pot, and a myriad of substances became my escape from the turmoil that plagued my inner self. The promising student I once was slipped away, replaced by a sense of worthlessness and the increased fear of judgment from others. Skipping school continued to be a regular occurrence, driven by my insecurities and the nagging belief that I was destined to be a failure. In my senior year, I succumbed to that belief and dropped out, opting instead to enter the workforce in 1972. It would be several years later when I finally obtained my GED.

When it was time to get my driver's test, I was so afraid of failing I let someone else take my test. I thought I was that slick. This fueled my behavior and ridiculous decisions as the years of learning to manipulate others became a skilled craft.

Yet it was fear masking itself as this legend that allowed the coward within me to move forward. This fear kept me from seeking help. I hid it well and the only person who knew was me. In my mind I built myself into something I wasn't. Even my brother didn't see it, calling me his "hero", while drugs and alcohol continued drowning out my deep inner reality.

The tumult in our family continued the following year. My brother joined the Navy, filled with hope and aspirations, only to be discharged shortly after due to his behavior. This was a huge disappointment to my mother and to our reputation. It became a sobering moment for me. I paused to question our status, but fell right back into the dark underbelly of our neighborhood where death was a constant threat.

There were four of us in the pack, our camaraderie bound by the thrill of thievery. But destiny had its own hand to deal, leading some down paths from which there was no return. Two of my childhood accomplices found themselves ensnared in life sentences; their dreams confined to the stark walls of prison cells. Another, drawn by the gravity of his own demons, wrestled with a sentence of 22 years for a crime that left scars beyond the physical.

In the heart of this tangled web I stood, a kindred spirit marked by a different compass. Amid the rush of adrenaline, and the lure of quick gains, my heart refused to align completely with the dark malevolence. While my peers danced with crime, I hesitated on the precipice, a silent guardian of the good that yet resided within me. A kind heart, beating to a different rhythm, held me back from stepping onto a path of irreversible darkness. It was this tenderness, this unwavering compassion, that acted as a counterweight to the pull of deviance.

In the labyrinth of our block, where life's stories were etched onto every wall and alleyway, fate cast its dice with an unforgiving hand. Three figures, once familiar faces in our shared childhood, found themselves painted into the darkest corner of existence—death row. Among them, two were sentenced to a fate that defied all human understanding—execution. These were not the stories whispered by distant strangers: these were lives I had watched unfold, like a series of chapters, lives that had intertwined with mine in classrooms, playgrounds and endless summer evenings.

I couldn't help but feel the cold touch of mortality tracing its fingers along the contours of my own life. Death, it seemed, had become another unwanted companion, haunting my steps as a reminder of the fragility that underpins our human lives. Those who had laughed, played, and dreamed alongside me were now ensnared by the inexorable march towards an untimely end. The weight of their fates pressed up on my shoulders, a stark reminder of life, so unpredictable in nature.

During these unfolding tragedies, I sought solace in the realization that while I walked a parallel path with those now condemned, my choices had diverted my trajectory. A sense of survivor's guilt mingled with the pain, reminding me that life can pivot on the tiniest of decisions, the slightest shifts in circumstance. As I stood there both a witness and a participant in this heart-wrenching drama, I understood that the presence of death in my story was a call to embrace life's fleeting moments, to hold close the ones we love, and to strive for a legacy that defies the shadows that loom on our shared horizon.

As I look back upon those chapters in my life, I recognize the delicate balance that defined our trajectories. The choices we made, the paths we walked, shaped our destinies in ways we could not fully comprehend in those formative years. My heart's resistance to cruelty and violence, its insistent call towards empathy, spared me from the shackles that ensnared my companions. It was this beacon of compassion that, even during darkness, held the promise of redemption, reminding me that no matter how far down the wrong path one may wander, there is always a glimmer of light waiting to lead us home.

FOUR
The Unraveling of the Family

In the shadowy theater of our lives, my mother emerged as an unlikely guardian against the encroaching darkness. Despite the suffocating veil of violence and criminality that draped over our neighborhood, she wielded a protective shield around my brothers and me, deflecting the poisoned arrows aiming to lure us into the embrace of the underworld. The clashes between my mother and stepfather, fierce and volatile, seemed to be as predictable as an approaching rainstorm.

Standing as witnesses, we sensed the impending tempest and warned him, like mournful prophets, "Lee, you know this won't end well."

But as the turmoil continued to whirl around us, my desperation reached a breaking point at the age of 17. Unable to bear the sight of my mother's enduring agony any longer, I added a chilling proposition, a pact of desperation between a son and a mother bound by shared suffering. "Mom," I whispered, "Let me do this. Let me put an end to his cruelty. I can't bear to see you suffer. Let me kill him."

Together, we etched out a plan. She would orchestrate the chaos, and I would play the role of the executor before vanishing into the night. But when the fateful hour arrived, my heart proved weaker than my convictions. The chilling truth that my soul recoiled from the brink of such brutality cast a shadow on my resolve.

My mother, though relieved by my moral pause, bore a nuanced resentment towards her sons, those who had been willing to dance with the devil for her sake.

Still, we implored her to flee, to abandon that haunted home and seek sanctuary elsewhere. As fate would have it, mere months later, the stage was set once more, this time with no rehearsal, no script to follow. My mother and unwitting heroine stood facing the abyss with a bravery only desperation can birth.

My stepfather stormed into the house with anger and menace exuding from every pore. Believing he was alone with my mother, he brandished a weapon, a physical embodiment of the rage that had gripped him. My mother's voice echoed in the silence, a cry of defiance that shattered the tension. I moved and his attention turned toward me. She seized the moment, lunging at him with a courage born of desperation. The detonation of gunshots punctuated the chaos, my mother wounded but unbroken. A battle for life and freedom unfolded before my eyes as they grappled on the floor, locked in a final, fatal duel. In the midst of this life-and-death-struggle, my brother emerged from the shadows, wielding his own weapon. Six gunshots rent the air, and a man's life was extinguished.

As I fled the scene, my heart pounding in tandem with the footsteps echoing in my ears, I was plunged into a swirl of emotions. Upon returning minutes later, I was brought face-to-face with a scene of haunting finality—my stepfather's lifeless body lay sprawled as a macabre centerpiece. Police and paramedics wove through the scene like spectral dancers in this tragedy. The sight that met my eyes was chilling, but as the fog of shock lifted, I found solace in the knowledge that it wasn't my mother lying there. She had been whisked away to the hospital, her fate uncertain. Meanwhile, my brother, now shackled by handcuffs, was being escorted away, a tragic hero in the eyes of the law.

My mother initially faced murder charges and spent a few days in jail, followed by attending consistent Alcoholic Anonymous meetings. Eventually, my brother's actions were deemed self-defense, and he spent only a few weeks behind bars.

In the years that followed, the memories of that night were buried deep within, except for the indelible image of my stepfather's lifeless form. My mother's agony, my brother's courage, and my own flight from the chilling scene were threads that would forever be interwoven into the fabric of our story, a story where light struggled to pierce through the encroaching night, where love and violence were intricately blended, and where a family's journey through darkness revealed the strength of their bonds.

FIVE
The Chaos of Adult Life Begins

During those tumultuous times, I had already crossed paths with Sharon. We had engaged in a relationship while still in high school, and our connection had resulted in the birth of a daughter. Although we never married, we went on to have two more children while I served in the military starting in 1974. Despite the joys of parenthood, the image of that lifeless body of my stepfather lingered in my mind. It followed me into every room I entered, a constant reminder of a loss I couldn't fully comprehend. I held bitterness towards him for how he had treated my mother, but I also realized I had never truly grieved his passing.

Joining the military amid my own internal turmoil, I carried the weight of undiagnosed PTSD from the traumas of my childhood. I became entangled in fights and rebelled against authority, fueled by pent-up anger that had accumulated over the years. Adding to that was the anger from the civil rights movement, which had penetrated deep into my soul.

It wasn't long before I went AWOL for 90 days, declared a deserter during wartime. Remarkably, my mother turned me in, and I faced a court-martial. Yet, by some divine intervention, they chose not to discharge me, recognizing a glimmer of goodness within. For the remaining three years of my service, I continued to struggle with fights, disrespect, and bouts of intoxication.

Upon my release from the military in 1977, I briefly reunited with Sharon before once again leaving her and our three children behind. I entered a new relationship, got married and began working at Chrysler, following in my birth father's footsteps. I believed I was on the path to success, but the grip of alcohol held me tightly. I couldn't maintain employment, and soon I found myself in and out of jail, eventually spiraling into homelessness, abandoning my wife and one set of children.

Living on the streets became my reality for eight long years. In the midst of my marital troubles, I was involved with another woman and fathered two additional children.

Tragedy struck when one of my daughters suffered from crib death, a loss that haunted me for years. In my grief, I placed the blame on her mother, who, like me, battled addiction.

I was with a lot of women at this time, living a ruthless life, treating women like dirt. I was a deadbeat dad. Present in name only, doing the bare minimum. I was selfish and narcissistic.

I refused to be faithful in my relationships—always having a few women on the side.

In this heart of Little Harlem, aka "The Island" in Toledo, Ohio, I carved out my own peculiar niche in this gritty urban landscape. This place I called home was a world unto itself, a place where the clock never seemed to tick past midnight. On these city corners, we gathered, a motley crew of night owls and rebels who thrived in the shadows where the air was thick with the smell of cheap wine.

The streets were our playground, our workplace, living life on the edge. We filled up on liquid courage and locked arms in brotherhood, even as our fists occasionally found their mark in violent clashes. It was amidst these dimly lit alleys and neon-lit liquor stores that I wove the threads of my own destiny, becoming the unassuming puppeteer of a band of thieves, a guild known locally as the "boosters."

They came to me like moths drawn to the flickering flame of opportunity. Their voices would echo in the night, inquiring, "What do you need?" A simple question that held the promise of anything your heart desired, as long as you could pay for it.

I became the broker of the wants, needs, and desires between those who hungered and those who could meet their cravings. Orders flowed in those alleyways. I orchestrated these covert transactions with confidence, ensuring that needs were met, desires fulfilled, and debts settled.

Compensation was a currency of its own in our realm. The boosters plied their nimble trade, acquiring coveted goods through shadowy means, be it a bottle of Robitussin cough syrup for the desperate addict seeking solace in the chemicals of escape or more extravagant acquisitions for discerning clientele. I would collect the spoils of these nocturnal adventures, greasing the wheels of our operation, ensuring the gears of our underworld machine continued to turn.

It was a hustle, a delicate balance of risks and rewards, a web of dependencies spun to support our greed. The people of Little Harlem had their own economy, their own rules, and their own peculiar sense of justice. In these streets, I honed my skills as a master manipulator. In this world, where the line between right and wrong blurred with every passing transaction, I found my place, and it was a place like no other.

In the dead of night, the streets echoed with the roar of engines and the distant wail of sirens, perilous actions unfolding beneath the unforgiving gaze of streetlights. Cars raced down the cracked asphalt like streaks of lightning in the night. Before you knew it, windows would shatter under a hail of gunfire, muzzles flashing, briefly illuminating the faces of those who had embraced the path of violence.

One night, another grim story played out. A confrontation unfolded, swift and brutal, as a battered stop sign, once a symbol of caution, was turned into an instrument of reckoning. The stop sign was lifted and struck with a resounding thud, extinguishing a life. It happened right in front of the police, with complete disregard for authority, serving as a stark testament to the depths of lawlessness that had swallowed our streets.

Even the local car wash had a dark underbelly. Behind the image, suds and spray, a different kind of business flowed. One where drugs flowed like a toxic river and deals were sealed. In this underworld of transactions, a hustler held court, guarding his empire with ruthless determination.

The day came when a hustler, emboldened by the lure of illicit gains, dared to challenge this dominion, and it ignited a fuse that would burn with deadly consequences. A gunshot sounded, echoed through the car wash's cavernous interior, silencing the would-be usurper. The hustler hit the gangster who had tried to rob him.

But violence begets violence in the relentless cycles of the streets. A few days later, a car, its windows tinted like the eyes of a lurking predator, pulled up with chilling intent. The air grew heavy with anticipation; everyone knew what was coming. The score needed settling, debts demanded payment, and retribution was a coin with two faces. The night sky witnessed the grim exchange, a deadly transaction that bore the weight of vengeance. Gunfire erupted. We all knew who did it.

This was my life. I was sharp, street savvy, looked up to. I lived in the grips of alcohol and anger. When I was alone, I still didn't face myself, didn't see what I was, who I was. I would pick up another bottle and hold my own.

Somehow God held on to me. Somehow, He saw me.

SIX
The Allure of Drugs and Alcohol

Though my life was in shambles, I clung to moments of self-improvement. I attended school during the day and sought refuge in homeless shelters at night. In 1986, I sought treatment for the first time, hoping to salvage my job. However, my journey to recovery involved multiple stints in and out of treatment over the course of 13 years.

But in 1987, crack cocaine seized hold of my life, plunging me deeper into the abyss. Three years later, I found myself in prison, ensnared by an attempted trafficking charge stemming from a sting operation. Although I was not a dealer, I received a two-and-a-half-year sentence. I served 18 months behind bars, determined to leave drugs behind. Yet, by nightfall on the day of my release, the allure of crack had already drawn me back in. I can still recall the look of disappointment on my mother's face as she stood in the doorway, shaking her head at the sight of my relapse. I felt overwhelming guilt, but it did little to deter me. I continued to cycle in and out of treatment, trapped in the grips of addiction.

These were the darkest years of my life, punctuated by dangerous encounters and near-death experiences. I found myself in precarious situations, seemingly destined for a tragic end. One chilling episode involved venturing into the crack-infested projects, unaware that I was being lured into a trap—a setup for robbery or worse. A cousin intervened, rescuing me from the depths of that dangerous maze. "Ricky, what are you doing?" he questioned, pulling me away from the perilous path. His presence saved me from certain harm, reminding me once again of the guiding hand of a Higher Power.

Another incident unfolded when I became involved with a woman who had an eight-year-old daughter. While living together, the child accidentally hurt herself, and in a moment of misunderstanding, her aunt assumed that I had caused the injury. Swift retribution was sent my way, as her sons armed themselves with bats, ready to administer a violent punishment. I was forcibly ejected from their midst, forced to navigate a gauntlet of menacing men. To this day, I remain unsure why they refrained from causing me harm. The only explanation I can fathom is the miraculous intervention of God.

On another occasion, I found myself entangled in a dispute, with someone wrongly accusing me of being a snitch. They confronted me with a relentless determination to exact their revenge. I pleaded my innocence, and somehow, against all odds, I managed to convince them that I hadn't betrayed their trust. In a world where there is no mercy for informants, I escaped the brutal beating that awaited me.

I lived in what we called abandominiums. Condominiums that were abandoned, declared unfit for use and boarded up. As I sat on the porch, I would see the families drive by, going to church, and I'd wish that was me. My life was so dark all the time. Some nights I'd be up for three days at a time, feet hurting so bad from walking constantly. We all smelt like kerosene from the heaters the dope boys provided for us to keep warm in the empty buildings.

The dealers would wait for customers to come by to get their dope, sometimes selling artificial dope called dummies. The dealers would hide for a few hours, knowing when the customers realized they were tricked, they wouldn't be brave enough to get out in those streets; customers would most often choose to accept their losses. Of course, there was a flip side to that—someone in a car could race by and snatch the dealers' bag and be off with it. For this they would get a relentless beating. I watched many of them. I didn't participate in this, I wasn't a dope boy.

I was a crackhead and didn't deal. I would, however, trick folks into giving me their money and run off. Some of my friends got two or three beatings, as they ran off with the dope boy's stuff. They would be pursued, knocked out, be brought back to consciousness, and then beaten again. We lived this rhythm in the streets day in and day out.

I did things I never thought I would do, especially stealing money from my mom, which amounted to about $800. When mom drank, she slept hard. One desperate night I abandoned my street and snuck into her home. I knew she had a little box under her bed, and I crawled in like an infantry man. I took some bills, crawled out, and ran down the street. I soon realized I had eight one hundred-dollar bills. I was horrified at this, I did not want to do this! Yet, I couldn't put it back, even when she blamed my brother for taking her money. I couldn't tell her. I was so petrified of her wrath! I held it deep inside for a long time. Eventually during my second year of being sober I made amends, and I took her money back. She was stunned as she never suspected me, yet she understood. I had to confess that I had stolen many times in small amounts from her. All was forgiven.

Once again, I recognized the hand of God protecting me in the face of so many moments of imminent danger.

SEVEN
The Process of Recovery

Amidst my journey of recovery, I found solace in the rooms of Alcoholics Anonymous. It was there that I crossed paths with Rosa, a beacon of strength and wisdom with fifteen years of sobriety under her belt. We connected, and in 1997, we joined our lives in marriage. The path to transformation led me to Prospect House in Cincinnati, a place where I could reside if I remained committed to personal growth. I delved into my studies, pursuing an Associate Mechanical Engineering degree at Cincinnati State, followed by a Bachelor's degree in Substance Abuse Counseling. Eventually, I earned a Master's degree in social work, specializing in Mental Health.

Sobriety became my anchor, and I embraced a complete turnaround. I actively participated in Alcoholics Anonymous, sponsoring others on their own journeys to recovery. However, my relationship with Rosa faced its own challenges, and we separated for a few years before amicably divorcing in 2007. We remained grateful for the lasting friendship we maintained.

True transformation, the kind that touches the depths of one's soul, doesn't unfold in the blink of an eye. It's a winding journey, often beset with detours that stretch far into the horizon. I, too, found myself ensnared in the labyrinthine corridors of self-deception, a prisoner to the notion that I was a legend, not in the eyes of the world, but in the recesses of my own mind.

My path to sobriety was neither swift nor linear. It twisted and turned, resembling a tangled web of half-truths and elusive epiphanies. Seven times I embarked on the arduous pilgrimage into the heart of treatment, each departure marked by the desperate hope for lasting change. Seven times, I gazed into the mirror of rehabilitation, determined to vanquish the demons that had ensnared me.

During those well-intentioned journeys, I found myself in the company of Wesley, a comrade in the battle for sobriety. Miraculously, he conquered his own demons, emerging from the abyss of addiction with newfound strength. His triumph served as a tantalizing glimpse of the redemption that lay within reach, had I dared to seize it.

Yet, there existed another facet of myself, an alter ego named Ricky. This was the coward, the saboteur, who emerged from the shadows whenever the scent of freedom lingered in the air. As soon as I took those tentative steps out of treatment's embrace, Ricky would stealthily resurface, luring me back into the abyss of addiction.

The eighth time was the charm, they say, and so it was for me. Over the course of those thirteen tumultuous years, each stint in treatment bore fragments of wisdom. But my self-proclaimed legendary status, the armor I wore to shield myself from the vulnerabilities of true change, proved stubbornly resilient. I clung to the illusion that I could conquer addiction without exposing the real me, without shattering the facade that had long concealed my pain.

Addiction whispers lies into your soul, convincing you that your worth is tethered to the poison coursing through your veins. It wages war against the very notion of seeking help, assuring you that isolation is the only path to survival. This sinister charade nearly cost me my life, since I was reluctant to allow anyone behind the barricades I had erected around my heart.

But in the end, change, real and enduring, could not be denied. The fortress crumbled, and I discovered that true strength lay not in the illusion of legendary status, but in the courage to embrace vulnerability. Sobriety, elusive for so long, emerged as a beacon of hope, casting aside the shadows, and revealing the authentic me, scarred but resilient, and finally, truly free.

Though I was sober, I still grappled with unhealthy behaviors. Infidelity tainted my early years of sobriety, and I engaged in harmful relationships with other women. While I managed to remain clean and steer clear of illegal activities, my personal growth required further work.

I shifted my focus to helping others, sharing my story in jails and prisons, hoping to inspire those who were still trapped in the grip of addiction. As time passed, my life continued to improve, and I learned to confront the haunting experiences of my past.

In 1998, I had two major breakthroughs. The first one was dealing with the death of my infant daughter, for which I had unjustly blamed her mother and myself. For seventeen years, I carried the weight of guilt until, in a moment of vulnerability during treatment, I penned a letter to my departed daughter, seeking her forgiveness. The act of sharing that letter with the group brought forth catharsis and released the shackles of guilt. Healing finally arrived.

The second was finally grieving the death of my stepfather. I had not wanted to make my mother angry for grieving his death, and I buried my emotions, yet I kept seeing his dead body year after year. Finally, during treatment, I realized why I kept seeing him—I had refused myself permission to grieve his loss. He had never hurt me directly, and my heart had held kindness toward him. I forgave myself for not grieving and acknowledging his place in my heart and the loss I felt.

During one of my AA meetings, I finally had the courage to share who I was. I unveiled the coward in me, the one who always built myself up to be someone I wasn't. I realized that this voice in me never allowed someone else to help me as I would tell myself, "They're not in my league." Yet my league was a coward's league. Driven by fear. AA helped me to see that I lived in self-centered fear, afraid of losing something I had or something I wanted. It created a blind obsession that was so destructive.

Over the course of my life, I have enjoyed the blessing of eight children from three different relationships, although my sixth-born son was taken by cancer in his thirties. I now find myself surrounded by the love of 31 grandchildren and 11 great-grandchildren, who, despite the physical distance, hold me dear in their hearts. However, my relationship with my youngest son remains strained, as he feels unable to forge a connection. The pain of this estrangement weighs heavily on me, and I long for a different outcome. But I find solace in the knowledge that I am exactly where I need to be at this moment.

Continuing my mission of helping others, I began working at the VA and, in 2013, I moved to Hinesville, Georgia. Retirement became a gateway to further service, and now I have the privilege of working with children at a grade school, making a difference in their lives.

Throughout my tumultuous journey, one constant presence has remained: God. There was a time when I doubted His existence, unable to believe in something I couldn't see, touch, or feel. My mother had been my guiding force for the longest time. Yet, as I embarked on my recovery journey in 1999, even as an agnostic, I couldn't ignore the truths spoken by those in the rooms of recovery. I made the conscious choice to "fake it till I make it." And as time passed, clarity began to emerge.

In the midst of my life's storms—the military, the struggles at home, the trials of the streets—I began to witness the hand of a Higher Power. Sobriety settled within me, and God started placing people in my path, offering glimpses of His presence. I marveled at the way He had guided and protected me throughout the years. I came to know that God had turned my life around, and I was filled with gratitude for His unwavering care.

Reflecting on my past, it's hard to believe that a man with three felonies, eight years of homelessness, and thirteen years of crack smoking, would find himself retiring from a government job, still serving his country. I often share my story with those who have been traumatized by life, assuring them not to despair over their records. I encourage them to focus on their own growth and leave the results in God's hands. For God had walked beside me through the darkest chapters of my life, molding me into a vessel of hope and inspiration for others.

This person, the coward, the legend in my own mind, is still there. The man who is now sober many years, giving, making a difference in the world—this is the real me. I don't regret the past, don't want to shut the door. I need to remember so I don't repeat it.

I had mindsets that held me captive, and I had to undergo a complete transformation in my thinking in order to recover and become who I was designed to be. I knew I had more to offer, knew I was better than someone waiting on the next crack-run, but in my mind I felt like a failure. Addiction smothers your best qualities and convinces you that you are less than worthy.

The greatest, the sweetest, the ultimate grounding factor is that I am a legend in God's mind! Because of using all these things to serve others, I've done the work, risen above it. It took courage and resilience to survive. Within me is brilliance, sensitivity that the Enemy tried to use to destroy me. God graciously placed people in my life at the right moments, to say the right things to get through to this fearful, proud man, to show me how to not just survive, but thrive and serve others for Him.

Are You Ready?

A Poem

God is the One who intervenes.
The One who loosens the grip
of the downward spiral on our lives.
Give Him a chance.
Don't give up on Him.
Do the work.

Look where your plans get you –
another fix, another failure?
My friend, are you done using?
Are you ready to surrender?

My Prayer for You

I am thankful for the many prayers prayed for me,
and for many I have had the opportunity to pray for.
I am thankful for the Serenity Prayer that has brought
release, life, and the grace of Jesus to me.
It is my prayer for you.

Serenity Prayer
by Reinhold Niebuhr

God grant me the serenity
To accept the things I cannot change;
Courage to change the things I can;
And wisdom to know the difference.
Living one day at a time;
Enjoying one moment at a time;
Accepting hardships as the pathway to peace;
Taking, as He did, this sinful world
As it is, not as I would have it;
Trusting that He will make things right
If I surrender to His Will;
So that I may be reasonably happy in this life
And supremely happy with Him
Forever and ever in the next.
Amen.

About the Author
Wesley Cole

Wesley Cole is a native of Toledo, Ohio. He was born and raised in the sixties and seventies, a period marked by social upheaval and cultural shifts with the Vietnam War, the Civil Rights Movement, the Hippie Movement, and the surge in marijuana and heroin use. This formed the backdrop against which Wesley's tumultuous life unfolded. His memoir, *A Legend in My Own Mind*, provides a poignant glimpse into a life entangled with the shadows of alcohol and drug addiction, a journey that ultimately led him to redemption.

Growing up in an environment saturated with drugs and crime, Wesley's early years were far from conventional. He sought solace in alcohol from a remarkably young age, the first taste of which lingered in his memory at the tender age of seven. He was caught in the vicious cycle of addiction, crime, incarceration, homelessness, and thirteen years of crack cocaine use. Wesley's existence seemed destined for despair. However, amidst the chaos, he discovered a profound source of strength. In 1999, a transformative moment occurred as

About the Author

he found salvation through the Grace of God, propelling him into the rooms of recovery.

God's presence became a guiding force, introducing transformative ideas, thoughts, and people into Wesley's life. Despite the challenges, Wesley's tireless determination led him to pursue higher education, earning degrees from Cincinnati State and the University of Cincinnati. His journey from the depths of alcohol, drugs, violence, and homelessness to a life of purpose and contribution is a testament to the resilience of the human spirit.

Wesley's narrative extends beyond personal triumph; it unfolds as a story of hope, courage, and unwavering belief for those ensnared in the clutches of despair. From the depths of addiction to the halls of academia, Wesley's story is an embodiment of the incredible love and grace that he believes God extends to all.

Today, Wesley resides in Allenhurst, Georgia, alongside his cherished wife, Michelle. His transformation from a life overshadowed by vice to one dedicated to helping others is reflected in his career as a Substance Abuse Counselor and Mental Health Therapist. Through his experiences, Wesley shares a compelling story that serves as a beacon of hope for those navigating the treacherous waters of addiction, showcasing the boundless love that, in his view, God reserves for every individual.

MARIGOLD PRESS BOOKS
A division of International School of Story

www.ingramcontent.com/pod-product-compliance
Lightning Source LLC
Chambersburg PA
CBHW052126070526
44586CB00016B/2105